RACE CAR DRIVERS
START YOUR ENGINES!

By Steele Filipek

with photographs

Grosset & Dunlap

Winning a NASCAR race is easy. The first car to cross the finish line after a certain number of laps around the course wins! Along the way, though, anything can go wrong. And there are a few rules to keep the drivers safe.

The cars can't be changed too much before or during a race. If they are, that's considered cheating. A team can be heavily penalized for altering their cars. The only people allowed in the car after

4

the start of the race are the driver and a doctor.

Drivers can't purposely damage another car during the race. They can get away with almost anything, though. That means blocking another car out of position. They can even drive danger-ously close behind another car to use the air spilling off of the front car to help give them a boost of speed. This is called drafting.

If there's an accident, all the racers have to slow down. This is so that emer-gency medical cars can get to the wreck quickly and safely. No driver can change position after the yellow (caution) flag has gone out. When the green flag is waved again, the drivers can continue.

After the race, points are assigned to all drivers and their teams depending on how they did in the race. The driver in first place almost always gets the most points. But other drivers can get points depending on where they finished (the better the position, the more points) or if they held the lead for a number of laps. When all of the races in the season are over, the points from every race are added up. The driver with the most points wins the series that he raced in.

Now that you know the rules of NASCAR, it's time to start your engines!

Ready to Race

Vroom! Forty-three drivers whip their cars across the starting line at the Homestead-Miami Speedway. Heading into the first turn, they speed up to 130 miles per hour. It's the Ford 400! It's hot! It's extreme! It's NASCAR.

This is the final race of the 2008 NASCAR season. From the first race in

Daytona over eight months ago, every race has led up to this one. After today, the driver and team with the most points will win NASCAR's biggest racing series—the Sprint Cup.

Over 100,000 fans are cheering in the stands. Tickets for this race have been sold out for weeks. Everybody has their favorite driver. Everybody thinks that their guy is going to win it all. But who will?

Dale Earnhardt Jr. makes an early move to get to the front of the pack. He slams his foot on the gas. Dale shifts up and cuts the corner as fast as he can without spinning out of control. He's making big moves and pushing cars out of his way. Dale started off the race in the number 22 spot. He has a long way to go if he wants to win this race.

But Kyle Busch won't be blocked out.

Even though he's only 23 years old—one of the youngest drivers in NASCAR—Kyle has led the standings for most of the year. Kyle cuts into the inside lane and keeps his position . . . for now.

Carl Edwards is right behind Kyle. His hands squeeze the wheel. His eyes scan the course, looking for a way to get out ahead. Carl needs to do well in this race. He's number 2 in overall points for the season. If he can win this race, and the leader drops far enough back, Carl will win the Sprint Cup Championship!

And Jimmie Johnson is driving the car in the lead. He's keeping up a good pace. He has the most points for this season. He doesn't even have to finish first in this race: He just has to finish close to first place and he'll have won his third Sprint Cup in a row.

But right now, it's still so early in the race. Anybody could come out on top.

Jimmie Johnson #48 and Dale Earnhardt Jr. #88 race side by side.

There's big prize money at stake for the person who comes in first: over $365,000 for the winner! All of the drivers' previous races this season are just a blur to them now. The 2008 Sprint Cup Championship is up for grabs. These drivers have been working their way up to this race since they first imagined driving in the NASCAR league. Let's find out more about how these four champion drivers got to this very moment.

Like Father, Like Son

Back in 2004, Dale Earnhardt Jr. was worried about the Daytona 500. That race is always the first in the NASCAR season, so it's important to do well. But for Dale, it was even more important.

His father, Dale Sr., was one of NASCAR's greatest drivers. And in 2001, while driving at Daytona, Dale Sr. crashed

Dale Earnhardt Jr. stands with his father Dale Earnhardt Sr. before a race in 2000.

his car and died. In 1998, Dale Sr. won his first race at Daytona. So that raceway had special meaning for Dale Jr.

Even though Dale really wanted to win the 2004 Daytona 500, he had been struggling on the race course. But when Dale got into his #8 car the day of the race, he focused on one thing: victory.

All of Dale's other awards and accomplishments seemed far away as he sat in the car with his hands on the wheel. He won many races before; he even won the Nationwide Series twice. And off the racetrack, he was a star, too. He voiced the character Junior in the Disney movie *Cars*, and appeared in music videos. But right then, all that mattered was the race.

The race started out like every other: fast! Jeff Gordon, John Andretti,

Jimmie Johnson, and many other drivers were all hungry for their first win of the season. Soon, they were pushing their cars over 170 mph. That means they could cover the length of a football field in one second!

But Tony Stewart wasn't going to make it easy for anyone. The lead changed between nine drivers 25 times before Tony swooped in front. For the next 97 laps of the 2.5 mile-long track, Tony was number one.

Dale didn't give up. Through four

Dale Earnhardt Jr. #8 passes Tony Stewart #20 with only a few laps to go at the 2004 Daytona 500.

crashes on the course—one in which 11 cars smashed into each other—Dale kept his cool. The number of cars dwindled to 21. That's when Dale finally had a chance to make his move.

With just 180 laps to go, Dale pushed his car as hard as he could and pulled up behind Tony. The two dodged and weaved for nearly a lap. Finally, Dale scooted past Tony to lead the race.

But Tony wasn't going down without a fight. Lap 199 came and went. Dale was still ahead of Tony, but not by much. Over three hours had passed since the beginning of the race. Dale was tired. But then there were only two miles left. Then one.

Then none.

The checkered flag whipped in the air as Dale crossed the finish line. He did it! He won the Daytona 500! Dale took

Dale Earnhardt Jr. raises his trophy after winning the race.

his victory lap. When he pulled over to the side, his racing team mobbed him in celebration.

For a man who grew up racing cars and watching his father win races, this was a dream come true. Dale had seen it all: racing go-karts as a teenager, buying his first car with his brother, and breaking into NASCAR at the age of 25. Winning Daytona that year made Dale feel like he was three years old again: messing around in the oil spills and dreaming of being a racer like his father. And now he was.

Big Winner

Jimmie Johnson didn't have a famous father like Dale. But he didn't need one, either. He drove in offtrack racing for years, in SODA, and SCORE International. When he started racing on pavement, he even won the American Speed Association's Rookie of the League award. At the same time, he was reporting on the American Speed Association (ASA) for ESPN.

It wasn't long before Jimmie made the jump from offtrack racing to NASCAR.

Jimmie Johnson gets ready to race.

He'd won six championships with the ASA and had finished in the top 3 in over 100 races. Finally, in 2002, when Jimmie was 27 years old, he made it into the Sprint Cup. He went on to win more points in his first season than any other rookie in history. Superstardom was just around the corner.

And now, four years after his amazing rookie year, Jimmie was about to fight for the biggest race of his life.

Jimmie Johnson, driver of the #48 Lowe's Chevrolet Monte Carlo, is pushed down the pit lane by his pit crew.

The race? The 2006 Aaron's 499. The place? Talladega Raceway, one of the most famous courses in the world. All of the famous NASCAR drivers have raced there: Jeff Gordon, Richard Petty, and Mario Andretti, to name a few. And now, Jimmie Johnson was one of them.

The race was scheduled for Sunday April 30, but it was rained out. All the drivers could do was wait for the skies to clear up. Jimmie tried to relax and stay calm. After all, he knew how to win races.

But this race was different. If Jimmie won the 2006 Aaron's 499, he'd be only the eighth person to ever win a career Grand Slam. A Grand Slam is when a racer wins each of the top four races on the Sprint Cup schedule: The Daytona 500, the Coca-Cola 600, the MD Southern 500, and the Aaron's 499.

Each of these top races has something special about them. The Daytona 500 gives out the most money and is the first race on the NASCAR schedule. The Coca-Cola 600 is the longest race at 600 miles long. The MD Southern 500 is the oldest 500-mile race, dating back to 1950. And the Aaron's 499 is the fastest, with the highest average speed for racers. To win, a driver had to be one of the best in the league.

On Monday, the rain stopped. The race was on. Jimmie jumped into his car and tore off down the track.

With cars moving at 190 mph, only a few drivers were able to handle driving at such a speed. Several cars quickly broke down from driving so fast. Some drivers crashed into the wall or into other cars. Jimmie weaved in and out of the lanes, avoiding danger. Slowly he gained ground.

With 15 laps to go, there was another crash. Denny Hamlin spun out of control and took several cars with him. Jimmie just managed to avoid the crash by picking up speed out of the turn. Now, with fewer cars on the course, it was easier for Jimmie to move. Once the wreckage was cleared, he sprung up to the front of the pack.

Brian Vickers was in the lead, and Tony Stewart wasn't far behind him.

Neither driver was going to give up first place without a fight. Like Jimmie, Brian and Tony had been fighting all year for a good spot in the standings. If Jimmie was going to win, Brian and Tony were going to make him earn it.

At the beginning of the final lap, Jimmie passed Brian on a curve and slid into first place. Tony tried to make a move, but it was too late. Jimmie finished first. As he stepped out of his car, Jimmie knew that not only had he won the race, he had won the Grand Slam!

Jimmie went on to win the 2006 Sprint Cup. The win at Talladega was just one of five victories for him that year. In 2007, when he won the Series again, Jimmie won 10 more races.

But the Aaron's 499 stood out the most to Jimmie. He defeated Brian Vickers and Tony Stewart: two of NASCAR's major drivers at that time. Johnson made history by winning two Sprint Cup Series in a row. There wasn't any doubt: Jimmie Johnson had become a legend.

Jimmie Johnson poses for photographers after winning the Aaron's 499.

A Backflip for Victory

Jimmie Johnson wasn't the only driver looking to make his mark on the NASCAR world. Around the same time that Jimmie was winning race after race, another driver named Carl Edwards stepped into the racing spotlight. His grand entrance into the Sprint Cup was at the Golden Corral 500 in 2005. Carl knew that the best way to make a name for himself was to beat one of NASCAR's best drivers on the scene at the time. He wanted to beat Jimmie Johnson.

Carl is known as much for what he's done off the race course as what he's done on it. He has appeared on the cover of *Men's Health* magazine, produced music, and guest starred on several TV shows. And the backflip that Carl does off the hood of his car after every victory is known throughout NASCAR.

But he knew that his fun personality and backflips wouldn't help him win races, especially one like the Golden Corral. To win, he'd have to use all his skills and talent. This was one of NASCAR's toughest races.

Carl Edwards does a backflip as he celebrates winning the 2008 Nationwide Ford 300.

From the start, Carl had his work cut out for him. He didn't have a good start position and had to claw his way up toward the front.

Carl was determined to win the race. But a lot of people had their doubts. Carl was a small-town guy, who had raced in a bunch of small-time races. Although Carl won on dozens of courses, he found it hard to break into NASCAR.

Carl's father, a dirt track racer in the Midwest, taught him never to give up. So Carl kept working. Although racing was in his dreams, Carl went to and graduated from college. He even became a substitute teacher. But he never stopped dreaming about making it big in NASCAR.

Finally, in 2001, Carl got his big break. MB Motorsports hired Carl to race in seven races for the Craftsman Truck

2003 Rookies of the Year: Craftsman Truck Series winner Carl Edwards, Winston Cup Series winner Jamie McMurray, and Busch Series winner David Stremme.

Series. In 2003 he was named Rookie of the Year for that series.

But to secure his place in the world of NASCAR, Carl needed to join a team. Luckily, Roush Fenway Racing liked what they saw and hired Carl as a full-time driver.

Two years later, at the 2005 Golden Corral 500, Carl was running out of time in the race. Carl began using all of the tricks he learned while racing in the

Nationwide and Craftsman Truck Series. He got himself closer to first place on the track by weaving between the cars. He even nudged some drivers closer to the edge of the track so he could push past them. He didn't break the rules, but he did race tough.

Soon Carl was near the front of the pack. Going into the final lap, Carl was just a car length behind Jimmie Johnson for the lead. Jimmie tried to stay ahead, but Carl managed to get closer and closer. By the last turn, Carl pulled up beside Jimmie. With only a quarter-mile to go, the two were neck and neck!

The two cars crossed the line in a near photo finish! But Carl came out the winner.

It was one of the closest races of the year! Carl beat out Jimmie by just .028

seconds! Carl had done it. He'd won his first Sprint Cup race! He was now a big-shot Sprint Cup driver.

Carl celebrated the race like he always did: with a backflip.

Young Star, Fast Car

Kyle Busch, racing in the 2005 Sony HD 500, took a sharp turn heading into the pit. He needed more fuel and new tires, but he didn't want to waste too much time. He'd been gaining on first place and

Busch's pit crew refuels his car before he goes on to win the 2005 Sony HD 500.

needed to get back out onto the course. He pulled into the pit and, in a flash, his crew went to work. They pumped gas into the car's tank. They jacked up the car, put new tires on, and slammed it back down. Kyle took a drink of water, and was off again. It all took less than ten seconds.

This car was a lot different than the cars Kyle used to drive when he was younger. Back when he was a kid, he raced go-karts in his hometown of Las Vegas. Kyle was hooked. He needed to race.

Kyle worked his way up the ranks on the way to NASCAR, just like every-body else. Kurt, his brother, even let Kyle be the crew chief on his dwarf car racing team. He wasn't just being nice, though. Kyle was good at fixing cars in the pit.

Soon, after he'd learned everything he could in the pit, Kyle started to race. He didn't just race cars: He also drove trucks, go-karts, and everything else with a motor. By the time he was 16, he broke into NASCAR by racing trucks in the Craftsman Truck Series. It seemed like everything was going Kyle's way.

But just as Kyle got his foot in the

Kyle Busch stands with his brother, Kurt.

door and began driving in NASCAR races, the league changed its rules: They made it illegal for anyone under the age of 18 to race cars. Kyle, being only 16, had to stop racing in the NASCAR league immediately. He was devastated. So when he was allowed back in at the age of 18, he worked hard in every race to show everyone just how good he was.

The 2005 Sony HD 500 wasn't going to be an easy race for Kyle to win. It was a good day for racing—not too hot, no rain—but that just made it an even course for everybody. No driver had an advantage. Kyle swerved through a line of cars and pulled into a better position.

Then, Kyle caught a break. He passed into the first spot, and then a wreck happened behind him on the course. No one was seriously injured, but all of the

drivers were locked into their spots. As the 500-mile marker came and went, it seemed like Kyle was going to win the race.

But a new rule gave Greg Biffle, the driver right behind Kyle, one more chance to pull ahead into first place. The rule stated that once the wreckage was cleared, two more laps would be raced, no matter how many times the cars had circled the track during the caution period. So, even though Kyle was in first place when the race hit 500 miles, it meant he still had to keep it for two more laps.

The cars circled the track at a slow pace, waiting for the signal that they could pick up their speed and try to pass each other on the course. The wreck took a long time to clear. Kyle sweated in his car. If he won this race, he'd be the youngest driver to ever win a Sprint Cup event.

Finally, the green flag was flown. The race was back on! Kyle, Greg, and the rest of the drivers sped up, shifted gears, and got back up to speed. They zoomed around the track and one lap passed quickly. The white flag went out, and then it was Kyle's turn to shine.

Greg jockeyed for position. Kyle kept pace in front of him. It was a dangerous spot to be in for Greg and a bad spot to be in for Kyle. Greg could use the air coming off of Kyle's car for a boost. But with so little track left, Kyle had to hang on. Greg tried to pull ahead, but Kyle blocked him. And then the two were on the last leg of the track, rocketing toward the finish line.

The checkered flag came down . . . Kyle had done it! He became the youngest NASCAR driver to win a Sprint Cup race!

Kyle's victory was definitely the biggest accomplishment in his life so far. Even though as a teenager he had already graduated high school with honors and won 60 races in three years racing Legends Cars. But his first Sprint Cup win was special because it proved that Kyle had the skill to compete against the best NASCAR drivers in the league.

The Sony HD 500 was just the first race Kyle won that year. He went on to

place first in four others, a record for a rookie driver. He won Rookie of the Year honors, and got even better the next year.

Kyle didn't win the 2005 Sprint Cup, though. He didn't do it in the next season, either. Kyle's still pushing for it, though by 2008, he would lead the Sprint Cup in points for most of the year. But then he fell behind, and it would take a miracle for him to win.

It all came down to one race in November . . . the Ford 400. Let's check back on the race where we started and see how our four drivers are doing!

One Lap to Go...

Back at the 2008 Ford 400, the white flag is out! It's the final lap! The day is winding down, but the cars are speeding up! This is their last chance!

Dale Earnhardt Jr. never even made it that far. He had problems with his wheel bearings on lap 246 and had to pull out.

Kyle Busch is still racing. Even though he is going at nearly 180 miles per hour,

Carl Edwards crossing the finish line to win the 2008 Sprint Cup Series Ford 400.

he won't be able to make it up to the top racers in time. He's almost a full lap behind the lead drivers.

And who are those leaders? Kevin Harvick and . . . Carl Edwards!

Carl has had an amazing race. He started off in the fourth position and managed to stay in a good spot the entire race! He even led the track for 157 laps! But that won't matter if he can't stay in front of Kevin for another couple of miles. He's raced through exhaustion and car wrecks on the course. If he can just hold out . . .

Kevin tries to make a move, but Carl manages to hang on. There's no room to move. They race into the final lap. No one can touch them now.

Kevin and Carl are separated by only a few hundredths of a second. The pavement underneath them is a blur. But Carl is still ahead!

The checkered flag is thrown! Carl Edwards has won the final race of the season. In a flash, the 2008 NASCAR Sprint Cup Series is over. Carl Edwards has the victory for this race . . .

But the real winner of the 2008 season is Jimmie Johnson. He finished 15th in the race, but that gave him enough points to win the Sprint Cup! It's his third in a row, tying the record set by Cale

Yarborough 30 years ago. Carl's backflip off the hood of his car is lost in the commotion. Jimmie has done it again!

For Carl Edwards, Kyle Busch, and Dale Earnhardt Jr., there's always next year. There are a lot of races, and none of these drivers is slowing down—not when they have their dreams to fuel them into the future.

Jimmie Johnson, owner Rick Hendrick, wife Chandra Johnson, and crew chief Chad Knaus pose with the Sprint Cup trophy!

NASCAR's Revved-Up Rules and Terms

American Speed Association: The ASA was a racing league like NASCAR. It featured paved courses, unlike the dirt courses of many other leagues. Many drivers got their start in this league, but it ended in 2004.

Camping World Truck Series: A NASCAR series in which drivers race modified trucks instead of stock cars. For a long time, this was called the Craftsman Truck Series.

Caution: A term used when the yellow flag is flown. This means that drivers must be careful. There could be wreckage on the track or an oil slick. Drivers must slow down, remain on the track, and not pass anybody until the green flag is flown again.

Checkered flag: A flag that is flown at the end of the race.

Crew: All the mechanics and managers who work in the pit.

Crew chief: The leader of the mechanics and managers. He or she oversees all of the work done in the pit and on the course to make sure things are going well.

Dwarf car: Similar to a miniature stock car, but can be enhanced to race at very high (100+ mph) speeds. Like go-karts, many NASCAR drivers learn the basics of racing on these machines.

Green flag: The flag that is waved at the beginning of the race. It is also waved when regular racing can continue after a caution flag is waved.

Lap: One complete trip around a race-course.

NASCAR: The National Association for Stock Car Auto Racing. It's the largest racing league in North America. It has over 1,500 races per year.

Nationwide Series: This series of races features cars that are almost the same as the Sprint Cup series. Drivers on the Nationwide circuit are usually younger or more inexperienced than those in the Sprint Series. It's kind of like NASCAR's minor league. It used to be known as the Busch Series.

Pit: The area alongside the race course where a driver's crew waits to fix the car.

Points: Points are awarded to drivers in different ways: how they finished in the race (1st, 2nd, 3rd, . . .), how many laps they led for, and simply for completing the course. The driver with the most points at the end of the season wins the series that he races in.

Pole position: The first racing slot for a driver at the beginning of a race. This is usually determined by a brief race or time trial before the main race.

Racing team: A racing team is the entire group of people who work on a car (or cars). Most work in the pit, fixing the car. There are also two or three drivers (including racers and back-up drivers), the publicists, owners, and sponsors on the team. Many people work on the team to make sure everything goes smoothly.

SODA: The Short-course Off-road Drivers Association was a dirt track racing league that ran from the 1980s until 1997. It featured heavily modified automobiles—like trucks, buggy cars, and a few stock cars—that raced on off-road tracks.

SCORE International: One of the premier off-road racing leagues in the nation. It was founded in 1973 and continues to hold races for trucks, motorcross bikes, and other dirt track racing machines.

Stock car: Cars that are in NASCAR races. Unlike certain race cars, stock cars are not built only to race. They are modeled after cars already produced by major carmakers.

Sprint Cup: NASCAR's most popular racing division. All of the league's best drivers race in this division. The Sprint Cup season runs from February through November. It used to be called the NEXTEL Cup.

Yellow flag: The flag that is flown to tell drivers to take caution.

White flag: The White flag is flown to show drivers that they are on the final lap of the race.